THE HOW AND WHY WONDER BOOK OF

BUTTERFLIES AND MOTHS

Written by
RONALD N. ROOD

Illustrated by
CYNTHIA ILIFF KOEHLER
and ALVIN KOEHLER

Editorial Production
DONALD D. WOLF

Edited under the supervision of
Dr. Paul E. Blackwood
U. S. Office of Education
Washington, D. C.

Text and illustrations approved by
Oakes A. White
Brooklyn Children's Museum
Brooklyn, New York

SCHOOL EDITION

Charles E. Merrill Books, Inc.
By special arrangement with Wonder Books, Inc.

Introduction

The delicate beauty of moths and butterflies is to be seen not only in their fanciful colors but also in the marvelous changes they undergo as they develop from egg to adult. This *How and Why Wonder Book of Butterflies and Moths* presents many fascinating details about these two representatives of the insect family.

Scientists have observed several unifying themes that run all through nature. One of these is the great variety among living things. Variation in shape, size, color, odor and texture is widespread, even though things may seem similar in many ways.

Another theme observable throughout nature is constant change. Things grow and decay; materials burn or rust; the earth's surface builds up and erodes; the seasons change.

Still another theme is dependence and interaction among things in our universe. Every living thing depends on other living things and on the environment. Interdependence is a key word describing this theme. Discovering the ways that organisms depend on one another and on their environment makes a challenging study for scientists.

All of these themes — variety, change, interaction — are abundantly illustrated by the moths and butterflies as they live their similar yet infinitely varied patterns of life. Thus, *The How and Why Wonder Book of Butterflies and Moths* will help young readers develop an understanding of nature.

Collecting moths and butterflies is a hobby with many rewards, and this book gives specific directions for going about it. It should be useful both at home and at school to guide young entomologists in their pursuit of knowledge.

Paul E. Blackwood
U.S. Office of Education
Washington, D. C.

Library of Congress Catalogue Card Number: 63-9528

Contents

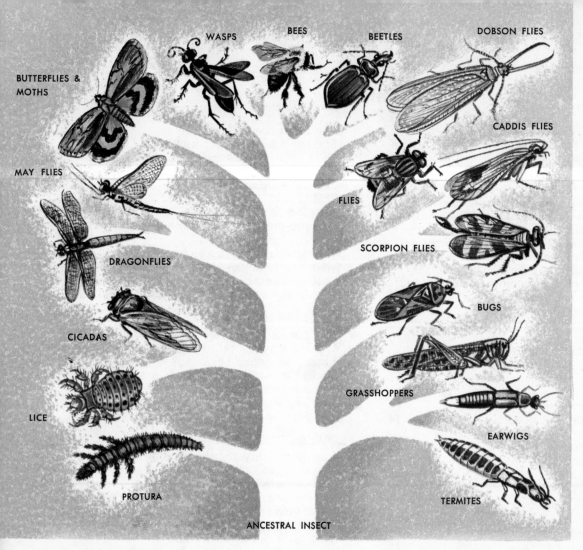

BUTTERFLIES & MOTHS

WASPS

BEES

BEETLES

DOBSON FLIES

CADDIS FLIES

MAY FLIES

FLIES

SCORPION FLIES

DRAGONFLIES

BUGS

CICADAS

GRASSHOPPERS

EARWIGS

LICE

TERMITES

PROTURA

ANCESTRAL INSECT

Butterflies and moths were, relatively speaking, latecomers to the family tree of insects, the class of animals to which they belong. But they made up for the loss of time. They are more numerous than most other insects; only the beetles have more known species.

Meeting Moths (And Butterflies, Too)

Scientists have classified all animals with broad com-

What is the place of butterflies and moths within the Animal Kingdom?

mon characteristics into groups called phyla, the phyla into classes, the classes into orders, the orders into families and the families into species. Butterflies and moths belong to the largest of the ten groups, the phylum of *arthropods* (segmented invertebrates, having jointed legs). Within the phylum they belong to the class of insects and form the order *Lepidoptera*. Nearly a

million species of insects have been identified, and scientists believe that many more exist unknown. Within the class of insects, the butterflies and moths form the second largest order, topped only by the order of the beetles which has over 250,000 known species.

Although no two kinds of insects are exactly alike, all of them have one thing in common. They have three distinct body sections. In fact, the name "insect" really means "In Sections."

The female bagworm moth doesn't have

What are the main parts of an insect? any wings. She looks more like a soft beetle than a moth. In fact, without its wings, any moth or butterfly is hard to tell from other insects. Its body is divided into the same three sections found in any insect on earth—head, thorax or chest, and abdomen or tail-section. Beetles and bees, aphids and ants, and crickets and cockroaches all have bodies made up of these same three parts.

Scientists have found fossils in the rocks

How long ago did moths and butterflies live? which tell them that moths and butterflies have been on earth at least fifty million years. Like other insects, they probably came from still earlier forms — perhaps 325 million years ago.

Some scientists think that these first insects were probably wingless creatures, perhaps something like a little insect known today as the *silver fish* or *firebrat*.

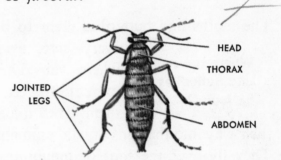

HEAD
THORAX
JOINTED LEGS
ABDOMEN

The wingless Spanworm shows that the butterflies have the same distinct parts that all insects have.

Trapped in amber millions of years ago, these well-preserved insects tell the story of the past.

Primitive reptiles, amphibians, and giant dragonflies were the inhabitants of the coal age swamps about two hundred and fifty million years ago.

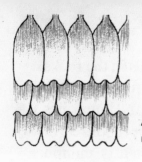

At right, the moth scales. Note the rugged edges as compared with the scales of the butterfly.

At left, typical arrangement of butterfly scales.

WHITE MOTH

HAWK MOTH

EMPEROR MOTH

HAIRSTREAK

BLUE

SWALLOW TAIL

CABBAGE BUTTERFLY

As the insects grew and developed over the millions of years, they took different shapes and sizes. Some became beetles and grasshoppers. Others became cockroaches, dragonflies, or wasps. Still others became moths and butterflies.

The moths and butterflies seem to be everywhere, even where you don't expect to find them. They make their way into the dens of wild animals. They fly over the tops of mountains. Some of their young drill through the wood of trees. Others make holes in clothes. A few live under water. Still others spend their entire lives in the tops of giant jungle trees, and never come to the ground. At least fifty kinds live in the frozen land of the Arctic Circle. Like the *mourning cloak,* they fly over the fields of snow.

Where can moths and butterflies be found?

Some moths have wings so huge that they are wider than this page. Others are so tiny that they spend most of their lives tunneling through the thin, flat world of a green leaf. In between are at least 100,000 different sizes.

How many kinds are there?

How long would it take you to count all the butterflies and moths that are known? If you started to write down the names of all the kinds at the rate of one per minute, it would take you nearly three months to complete the list.

Each one of these thousands of moths and butterflies has a story all its own. It would take a whole library of books to tell about them all. However, you will see that many parts of the story are the same for each one.

If you hold a butterfly or moth between your fingers, one of the first things you will discover is the powder on its wings. Under a magnifying glass this powder takes on fascinating shapes. It is powder no longer, but a mass of thousands of scales. They are shaped in a wonderful variety of patterns — some diamond-shaped, some like shields or spears, some oval, some round, some square. They lie on the wing like the shingles of a roof, often covering it entirely. These scales give strength and protection to the wing. In fact, scientists have named the moths and butterflies *Lepidoptera,* which means scaly-winged.

Why are moths and butterflies sometimes called scaly-wings?

Perhaps you have noticed that many insects have hairs on their bodies. Bumblebees are fuzzy. So are many flies. The powder on the wings of a moth or butterfly is really hair which has developed into scales by taking many flattened shapes.

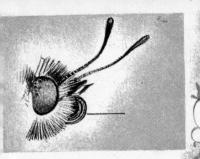

Closeup of the head of a butterfly, sucking tube (proboscis) coiled.

Moth approaching a flower with tube uncoiled to reach the nectar in the flower.

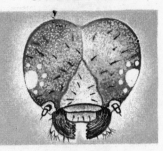

Most larvae (caterpillars) have chewing jaws instead of the proboscis of the adult insect.

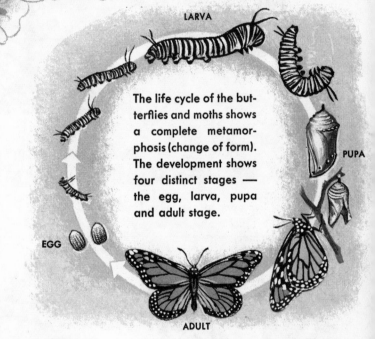

LARVA

The life cycle of the butterflies and moths shows a complete metamorphosis (change of form). The development shows four distinct stages — the egg, larva, pupa and adult stage.

EGG

PUPA

ADULT

If all the scales are taken off, there is usually no color left in the wings at all. There are hundreds and thousands of moth and butterfly patterns, all made by the color and arrangement of the scales. Some scales are colorless, but have fine lines on their surface. In the beautiful morpho butterflies of South America there may be 30,000 lines to the inch. Scales catch the light and break it up into rainbow colors.

What gives the wings their color?

Besides the scaly wings, butterflies and moths also have very strangely-shaped mouths. In place of jaws, they usually have a long, slender tube that works back and forth. When the tube is not in use it is coiled up under the head. The insect uncoils the little tube to get at the nectar at the bottom of a flower. Sometimes two or three butterflies may feed from a flower at once, like three people with straws all sipping from a single ice cream soda.

Why are moths and butterflies sometimes called tube-mouths?

It's hard to tell from observing a young moth or butterfly what form it will take when it becomes adult. The youngster does not look like its parents, for it is a wormlike creature called a *larva* or *caterpillar*. It has no wings. In place of the coiled tube-mouth, it has powerful chewing jaws. It creeps along on the edge of a leaf seeming to pay no attention to the insects flying above it.

What is a young butterfly like?

When fully grown, the caterpillar changes into something resembling a

7

RED SPOTTED PURPLE

BANDED PURPLE

The banded purple and red spotted purple are members of the Brush-footed family (Nymphalidae).

COMMA

CHECKERSPOT

GREAT SPANGLED FRITILLARY

DIANA FRITILLARY

ZEBRA BUTTERFLY

REGAL FRITILLARY

AMERICAN COPPER

EASTERN TAILED BLUE

PARNASSIUS

GREAT PURPLE HAIRSTREAK

MESOSEMIA GRANDIS

ALFALFA BUTTERFLY

BLACK SWALLOWTAIL

TIGER SWALLOWTAIL

TIGER SWALLOWTAIL
LARVA

ZEBRA
SWALLOWTAIL
LARVA

ZEBRA SWALLOWTAIL

FOREIGN RELATIVES

NORTHERN JUNGLE QUEEN
(SOUTH AMERICA)

DOG'S-HEAD BUTTERFLY
(A BOLIVIAN PIERID)

PAPILIO CHILDRENAE
(CENTRAL AMERICAN
RELATIVE OF THE
SWALLOWTAILS)

OX-EYED PANSY
(INDIA, AUSTRALIA)

UPPER SIDE

UNDERSIDE

CYMOTHOE SANGARIS
(AFRICAN NYMPHALID)

AGRIAS AMYDON (A SOUTH AMERICAN
MEMBER OF THE NYMPHALIDAE)

mummy. This is called a *pupa*. After a while, the pupa splits and the new adult crawls out. Now at last the moth or butterfly can be seen.

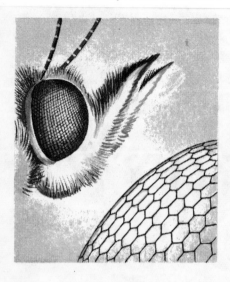

The compound eyes of butterflies and moths are made up of hundreds of six-sided lenses.

If you look at the head of an adult, you

How many eyes does an adult have?

find that it seems to be made up mostly of two huge eyes. These are called compound eyes, and are really composed of hundreds of tiny units or facets. One moth, known as a sphinx moth has 50,000 facets in its eyes. As if these were not enough, there may be two tiny single eyes just above the compound or many faceted ones.

Scientists think the compound eyes

see moving objects very well. They probably give a general picture of the world. The single eyes may be used for close-up viewing.

What does the world look like to a crea-

How does the world look to an insect?

ture with thousands of eyes? By working carefully, scientists have been able to take a photograph through an insect's compound eye. The resulting photograph is composed of thousands of dots. When viewed all together, these dots make a picture called a *mosaic*. If you want to see a mosaic picture look closely at a photograph in a newspaper under a magnifying glass. You will see that it, too, is made of thousands of dots. Perhaps this newspaper photograph is similar to what an insect sees.

How can you tell a moth from a butter-

How do moths and butterflies differ from each other?

fly? For one thing, moths usually have thicker bodies than butterflies. There is also a difference in the feelers or antennae, atop the head. Moths often have thick or feathery an-

If you compare the Cynthia moth (left) with the Papilio Columbus, a Cuban Swallowtail butterfly (right) you will see that the moth is thicker bodied and that the antennae are quite different from the butterfly.

GULF FRITILLARY BUTTERFLY (RESTING)

When a butterfly rests, its wings are vertical (folded up).
When a moth rests, its wings are horizontal (folded down).

EMPEROR MOTH (RESTING)

tennae. They generally come to a point at the tip. The antennae of butterflies are usually slender, and end in a little knob or swelling.

No matter what their shape, however, the antennae are wonderful organs. They can be used like little fingers to tell the shape and "feel" of objects. Perhaps they can detect sounds. They can also pick up odors in the air that are much too faint for our human noses. Some moths can detect odors coming from as far as five miles away.

What are the uses of the antennae?

Still another way to tell a moth from a butterfly is to look at them while at rest. Most moths rest with their wings flattened out, while butterflies usually rest with theirs pointing straight up. Butterflies usually fly

How else do moths and butterflies differ?

in the daytime and moths at night. Often, the wings and bodies of moths are fuzzier than those of butterflies. A moth fluttering at a window makes a little cloud of dust as thousands of scales break off its wings. Usually these scales do not grow back, so an old worn-out moth may actually have its wings partly bare.

Larvae of both moths and butterflies have fleshy little legs on their abdomen, called *prolegs*. The adult insects have all six legs and four wings crowded on the thorax. The abdomen of a female is often nothing more than a big bag containing hundreds of eggs. Her load of eggs may be so heavy that it can keep her from rising into the air.

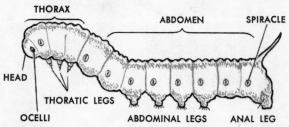

THORAX — ABDOMEN — SPIRACLE

HEAD

THORATIC LEGS

OCELLI — ABDOMINAL LEGS — ANAL LEG

Parts of moth larva (caterpillar) you should know.

11

POLYPHEMUS MOTH

IO MOTH

AMERICAN
COPPER
UNDERWING

COTTONWOOD
DAGGER

PINK SPOTTED HAWK MOTH

PROMETHIA MOTH
(MALE)

ACHEMON SPHINX

BLINDED SPHINX

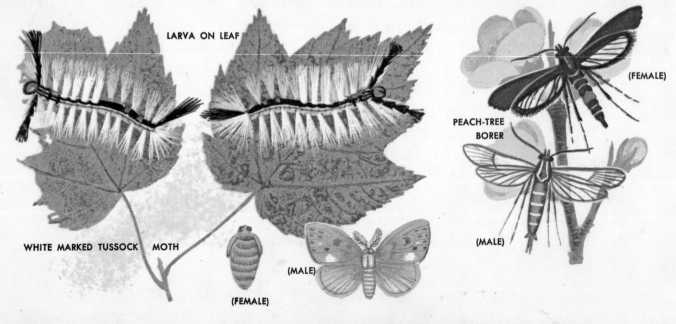

LARVA ON LEAF

(FEMALE)

PEACH-TREE
BORER

(MALE)

WHITE MARKED TUSSOCK MOTH

(FEMALE)

(MALE)

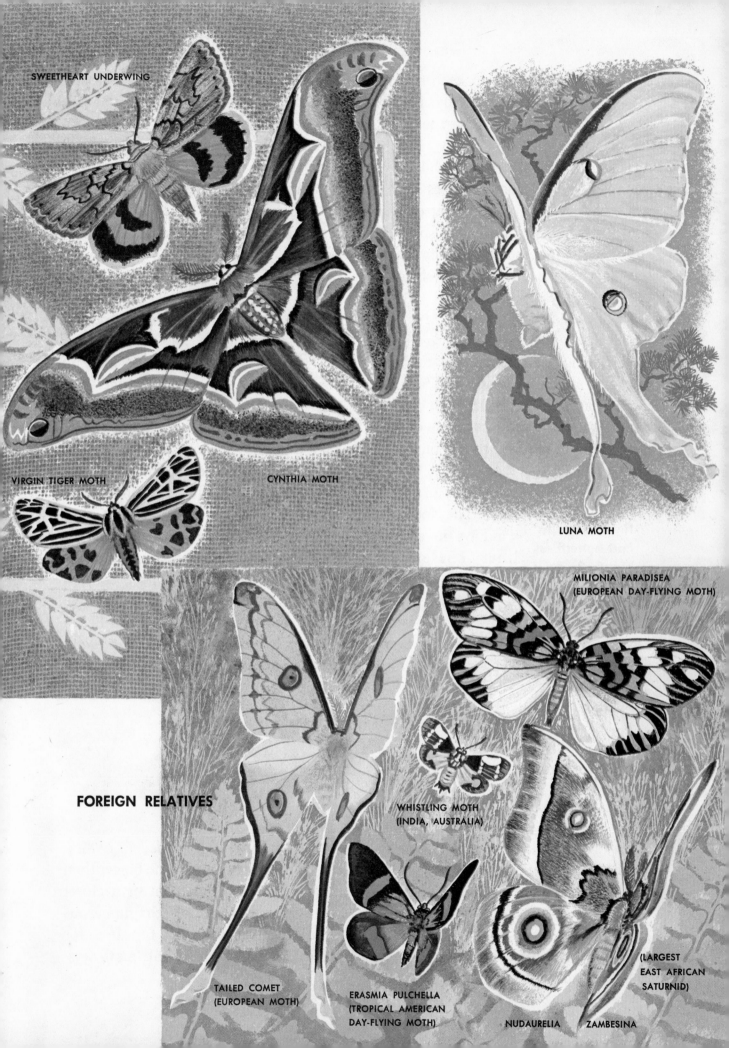

SWEETHEART UNDERWING

VIRGIN TIGER MOTH

CYNTHIA MOTH

LUNA MOTH

MILIONIA PARADISEA
(EUROPEAN DAY-FLYING MOTH)

WHISTLING MOTH
(INDIA, AUSTRALIA)

FOREIGN RELATIVES

TAILED COMET
(EUROPEAN MOTH)

ERASMIA PULCHELLA
(TROPICAL AMERICAN
DAY-FLYING MOTH)

(LARGEST
EAST AFRICAN
SATURNID)

NUDAURELIA   ZAMBESINA

How do insects grow? No matter how long you keep a moth or butterfly, its size will stay the same. Like other insects, all its growth takes place while it is young. The caterpillar becomes stuffed with food until its outer jacket or skin splits open. This jacket has to split, because it cannot stretch — any more than last year's shirt will stretch to fit this year's boy.

Under the old jacket is a new one, which is so soft that it is able to stretch for a few hours. The caterpillar's body swells as much as possible. Then the jacket hardens again. This process of *moulting* repeats in most larvae of butterflies and moths four-to-five times.

Along the sides of the body are little holes. They look like windows in an airliner. These holes are called *spiracles*. **How do moths and butterflies breathe?** They lead to thousands of tiny tubes within the insect's body. The tubes act as air-pipes. They branch into every part of the insect. They carry fresh air and get rid of waste air. Since insects have no real lungs, they do not breathe through a mouth or nose. This is lucky for a little caterpillar that lives at the edge of ponds. It spends much of its time with its head below water feeding on underwater plants. It feeds with its front end and breathes with the rest of its body.

There are other strange things about moths and butterflies. **How else do they differ from other creatures?** Like all insects they have no bones inside their bodies, which are protected by an outer jacket or *exo-skeleton*. Although they have a heart, there are no true arteries or veins. Blood, not red but green, yellow or colorless, flows through their hollow bodies and legs

Some butterflies have taste buds on their feet, so they can sample flowers they alight upon. Others have ears on their sides instead of on their heads. Sphinx moths sometimes squeak like a mouse when caught. A few caterpillars make a noise by grinding their jaws.

LARVA
MOULTING

Some Moth and Butterfly Families

Today's moths and butterflies are divided into many smaller groups, or families. You can tell the families apart by their wing-veins, colors, and habits. It is not possible to list all the families and their members, but a few of the ones you may meet are mentioned here.

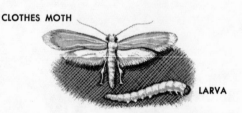

CLOTHES MOTH

LARVA

CLOTHES MOTHS, *Tineidae (Ti-NEE-i-dee)*. Tiny clothes moths, no bigger than a fly, sometimes burst out of a closet when it is opened. Their numerous larvae feed on wool and fur. It is for protection against them that "moth crystals" are made.

ADULT EUROPEAN CORNBORER LARVA

BAGWORM MOTHS, *Psychidae (SIK-i-dee)*. Their silken pouches, covered with twigs or evergreen needles, are sometimes very common on trees and shrubs. The pouch looks almost like a little pine cone moving slowly along the tree branches.

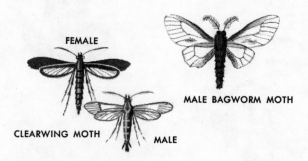

FEMALE
MALE BAGWORM MOTH
CLEARWING MOTH
MALE

CLEAR-WING MOTHS, *Aegeriidae (e-JER-i-dee)*. With few scales on their wings, they look like bees or wasps. Some are colored yellow and black, and may even pretend to sting. Their larvae are borers in peach trees and other kinds of plants.

CODLING MOTHS, *Pyralidae (Pi-RAL-i-dee)*. If you have ever bitten into a wormy apple, you have probably met the larva of the codling moth. The adult is a little brown moth which flies around lights in summer. The Mexican jumping

The larva of the Codling Moth is a widespread apple pest.

bean larva is in this family. The European corn borer, aquatic caterpillars, and the little wax moth of beehives are relatives of codling moths.

SPHINX or HAWK MOTHS, *Sphingidae (SFIN-geh-dee)*. These large, narrow-winged moths are streamlined for swift flight. The front wings may be beautifully marked in black, brown, and white. The hind wings may be pink, yellow, or several colors. Tomato hornworms are sphinx larvae.

MEASURING-WORM MOTHS, *Geometridae (JEE-a-MET-ri-dee)*. Inchworms, loopers, and measuring-worms are all larvae of this family. The adults, dainty like butterflies, have delicate markings on the light-colored wings.

FEMALE
MALE
FALL CANKERWORM

OWL MOTHS, *Noctuidae (Nok-TU-i-dee)*. This is the largest family of Lepidoptera, found all over the world, and characterized by their dusky tints and nocturnal habits. Cutworm moths, in this family, often feed on plants. The caterpillars of the cotton worm moth destroy the bolls on cotton plants.

CORN EARWORM LARVA

ISABELLA MOTH LARVA
THE WOOLLY BEAR CATERPILLAR

ISABELLA MOTH

SKIPPER

HICKORY HORNED DEVIL
MOTH AND CATERPILLAR

SKIPPER LARVA

EMPEROR MOTH
LARVA

SPICEBUSH SWALLOWTAIL
CATERPILLAR

EMPEROR MOTH

GYPSY MOTH
LARVA

PROMETHEA

GYPSY MOTH

MONARCH

PROMETHEA LARVA

MONARCH LARVA

ST. LAWRENCE TIGER

TIGER MOTHS, *Arctiidae (Ark-TEH-i-dee)*. These small moths may be beautifully marked like a tiger. They are not ferocious, however, but are named because of their color. The woolly bear caterpillar is a tiger moth larva.

MALE SILKWORM MOTH

SILKWORM MOTHS, *Saturniidae (Sat-UHRN-i-dee)*. Here are the giant cecropia, polyphemus, and luna moth. Most of these moths are large, furry, and have beautiful colors. The silkworm is also found in this family. Its moth is small and light-colored.

SKIPPERS, *Hesperiidae (Hes-PER-i-dee)*. Fast-flying little insects, the skippers look almost like a cross between butterflies and moths. Many skippers have a

ARCTIC SKIPPER AND LARVA

fringe of hair which looks like eyelashes above their compound eyes. Skipper larvae have a small neck which looks as if they were wearing a tight-fitting collar.

SWALLOWTAIL BUTTERFLIES AND PARNASSIANS, *Papilionidae (Pap-PIL-yon-i-dee)*. The swallowtails are a common sight in the country. They have two long "tails" like those of a barn swallow.

BLACK SWALLOWTAIL

MONARCH BUTTERFLIES, *Danaidae (Da-NAY-i-dee)*. The familiar orange and black monarch butterfly and its relatives are found over most of the world. It is known for its long migrations. The queen, also in this family, is chocolate brown and black.

MONARCH

WHITES AND SULFUR BUTTERFLIES, *Pieridae (Pe-ER-i-dee)*. This family includes the little sulphur and cabbage butterflies. Most of these are yellow or white. The dog face butterfly has a picture of a dog on its wings.

COMMON SULFUR BUTTERFLY

BRUSH-FOOTED BUTTERFLIES, *Nymphalidae (Nim-FAL-i-dee)*. This large family· has front legs which look like

RED ADMIRAL

little brushes. They usually walk with just the last two pair of legs. The family includes the mourning cloak, fritillaries, tortoise-shells, and admirals.

WESTERN PYGMY BLUE

BLUES, COPPERS AND HAIRSTREAKS, *Lycaenidae (Ly-SEN-i-dee)*. These are very small butterflies. Although often brown in color, they may have a beautiful blue glint to their wings. Some of the larvae of the blues feed on other insects. The hairstreaks and coppers belong to the same family.

There are still more families of moths and butterflies. In order to identify them you will need books to help you. Some can be identified from this book, but you may also wish to get other guides. A book store may help you to get them.

For thousands of people collecting butterflies and moths is an interesting hobby. The living insects are even more fascinating. The rest of this book tells a few of their wonderful stories.

The Great Awakening

MOURNING CLOAK
LARVA

It has been a long winter. Snow has been on the ground since late fall. There is not a sound in the woods. Everything seems to be waiting for the longer days of spring. The sun shines brightly on a patch of snow in a forest. Suddenly one of the last insects you would expect to see flying over a snowdrift appears. It is a brown butterfly, warmed by the rays of the sun. All winter it has been resting under a loose piece of bark, its wings tightly closed over its back. Now it flutters out for a few minutes. It is a mourning cloak butterfly, one of the first insects of spring.

There are thousands of other moths and butterflies around, but they are not yet visible. Many of them are still nothing but eggs, placed on a twig, or dropped on the leaves by their mothers last autumn. Other eggs have hatched and are now little caterpillars, curled tightly in the cold. Some of these have turned into pupae, or moth-and-butterfly-cases. They will emerge from their cases as butterflies or moths when the weather gets warm.

A few moths and butterflies from the East and Northeast have flown south for the winter. Some are just a few miles from their summer homes. Others have gone as far as Virginia or Missouri. A few have even gone to Florida or California. Many, however, stay in the northland. They are sleeping in a sheltered spot with folded wings. The mourning cloak is almost the only butterfly to be seen while snow is still on the ground.

It finds a broken tree branch. Sweet sap is running from it, and the little butterfly takes a drink. The sun is sinking. The mourning cloak hurries back to its shelter. Soon the temporary February thaw is over, and the earth becomes cold once more.

Every day, however, the sun grows stronger and the days get longer. The buds of the pussy willow begin to swell. Snow falls, but often melts in the noonday sun. Woodpeckers begin to drum their spring song by beating on hollow trees. Boys look for their baseball hats. Girls think about roller skating. Soon the mourning cloak butterfly is out again.

This time it may stay out all day. Now it is joined by other insects. Gnats fly in the bright sunshine. Stone flies come out of the icy water of the brook. Snow fleas jump on the snow. All of these insects are dark colored; thus, their bodies absorb the heat of the sun.

The great awakening after a long winter: the first butterflies over snowdrifts.

Then, when they are warmed, they begin to move around.

A few small moths called millers flutter in broad daylight. A red admiral butterfly opens her wings after the long sleep. The moths and butterflies join the mourning cloak near a drop of tree-sap. With the melting of the snow, the brook begins to rise. Soon it overflows its banks, carrying with it ice and snow.

At the base of a sunny rock a green bud appears, followed by another, and another. In a few days the first spring flower has opened.

The butterfly visits the flower. It finds a drop of sweet nectar deep in the blossom. As it flies away, it doesn't notice a little creature which climbs up on the young green leaves. It is a newly hatched caterpillar, no larger than a grain of salt. All winter it has waited for this day. Now it starts to nibble away at the edge of the leaf.

Spring has come to the plants and animals. It has also come to the world of moths and butterflies. The great awakening has begun.

Eggs by the Hundreds

How many eggs of butterflies and moths have you seen? They can be found in a number of places. Many are hidden under the bark of trees. Some are laid on the flat surfaces of rocks. Some moths and butterflies just scatter them as they fly; the eggs fall like tiny raindrops. If a moth gets caught inside a house, she may lay her eggs on the windowpane. The mourning cloak, like many others, lays her eggs in a little collar around the twig of a tree. When her caterpillars hatch, a supply of fresh green leaves will be at hand.

What do the eggs look like? The eggs come in many shapes. Some are star-shaped. Others look like little short-handled umbrellas. There are eggs with ridges, eggs with spines, and eggs with knobs and loops. There are sticky eggs and dry eggs, red eggs, yellow eggs, brown eggs, and white eggs. The round eggs may look like tiny pumpkins; the flat eggs may look like plates; the long ones look like miniature sausages.

How are eggs protected for winter? Each moth and butterfly has its own special type of egg. The gypsy moth lays a sticky mass of round eggs and covers them over with the hairs from her own body. They stay under this blanket all winter. The *tent* caterpillar moths cover their eggs with a foamy mass of glue. This hardens into a tough covering which keeps out snow and water.

Some spiny tailed moths poke a hole in a twig and lay their eggs inside. Many moths and butterflies just dart at the leaves and fly away; but they leave their moist eggs clinging to the plant.

How many eggs does a moth or butterfly lay? The number of eggs laid is different for different types of insects. Usually, each insect will lay two or three hundred eggs, but only a few will hatch.

Many eggs laid in the fall do not hatch in the cool fall weather. They will wait until spring. Sometimes, however, the weather stays warm for weeks. If the caterpillars began to crawl around on a warm November day, they would soon starve for lack of food. So nature has provided a wonderful safeguard to keep them from hatching too soon.

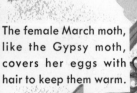

The female March moth, like the Gypsy moth, covers her eggs with hair to keep them warm.

EGGS OF EMPEROR MOTH

MOURNING CLOAK EGGS

EGGS OF CABBAGE BUTTERFLY

EGGS OF MONARCH

The safeguard works in this way. Unless many eggs first go through a period of freezing, they will not hatch, no matter how warm the weather. Thus, a cold winter day actually helps them get ready for hatching in the spring.

How long do eggs take to hatch?

Not all eggs take months before they hatch. A few days after the *cabbage* butterfly has laid her single, white eggs on the leaves of cabbages and turnips, the newly hatched green caterpillars are soon nibbling at their salad. The eggs of certain other moths take even less time. In fact, they hatch while they are still in the body of the mother. When she goes to lay her "eggs," they have already become tiny living caterpillars!

Many caterpillars can eat only certain plants. The mother seems to know which plants will make good food. She probably uses the sense of smell in her delicate antennae. She lays her eggs on plants which give off the proper odor. If she cannot find the exact plant, she will pick a close relative. Thus a clover moth may also lay her eggs on alfalfa, while a bean moth may lay her eggs on peas.

How does the mother know where to lay her eggs?

Scientists have found that they can fool moths by tricking their sense of smell. Cabbages, turnips, radishes, and broccoli all belong to the mustard family. By smearing mustard oil on paper, they can make cabbage butterflies lay their eggs on it. The corn earworm moth may lay her eggs on cloth soaked in corn oil, instead of corn silk.

The *tobacco sphinx* moth usually lays her eggs on tobacco plants. But if a pack of cigarettes is available, she may carefully place her eggs on the outside of the package!

Some of the eggs rest in strange cradles. *Peacock* moths lay their eggs on stinging nettles. *Cactus-borer* moths crawl over prickly spines to lay their eggs. The wax moth creeps into a beehive, even though the bees would kill her if they found her. Her newly born caterpillars will feed on the beeswax in the honeycomb.

Where can the eggs be found?

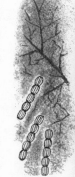

EGGS OF VIOLET TIP

The female yucca-moth pierces the flower of the yucca or *spanish-bayonet*. She then lays a few eggs with her sharp *ovipositor* or egg-laying organ and rolls a ball of pollen from another yucca flower around it so it will help her flower to form seeds. The seeds grow just in time to feed the new caterpillars.

Scientists know of no other way in which pollen can get from one yucca flower to another. Without the little white yucca moth, there would be no

CECROPIA EGGS

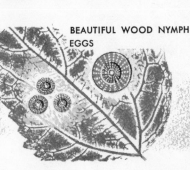

BEAUTIFUL WOOD NYMPH EGGS

ALL EGGS ARE VERY MUCH ENLARGED.

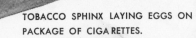

TOBACCO SPHINX LAYING EGGS ON PACKAGE OF CIGARETTES.

seeds. Since the caterpillar does not eat them all, there are always some seeds left over to grow new plants. (See illustration, page 39.)

What is a bagworm cradle? Bagworm eggs are in one of the strangest cradles of all. The female caterpillar makes a silken pouch and covers it with evergreen needles or twigs. Wherever she goes she pulls this pouch around, like a turtle with a shell. When she turns into a moth, she has no wings or legs and stays right in her pouch. Soon after laying her eggs, she dies. When the new caterpillars hatch, they must make their way out through their mother's pouch. Soon they start little bags of their own.

EGGS OF AMERICAN TENT CATERPILLAR MOTH.

How can you care for the eggs? If you find an egg mass under a bit of bark or wrapped around a winter twig, you may wonder how to take care of it. If you bring it inside where it is warm, you'll quickly find that you have made a mistake. Soon there will be tiny hungry caterpillars all over the room. Since many egg masses have several hundred eggs, it is better to leave them outside. They will not hatch in the cold air. You should put them in a box or jar, because birds and mice will eat them if they get a chance.

How can eggs be kept from hatching? To keep the eggs from hatching at all, put them in a "killing" jar. This is a jar with a little carbon tetrachloride in the bottom on a piece of cotton. (Directions for making it will be found in the last chapter of this book.) Leave the eggs in the jar for a day or two, to be sure they are dead.

Eggs can also be preserved by putting them in a sieve over a pan of boiling water. The hot steam will kill them in about five minutes. Steam sometimes discolors eggs or melts the waxy covering, and should be used with care.

How can eggs be displayed? Eggs can be displayed by pinning them to a little white card. They may also be saved in a small bottle. Be sure to write down where and when they were found. If possible, write down the kind of plant they were on. This is often a big help in identifying them later.

The eggs of the Bagworm are in the "cradle," made by the larva of this moth.

Larva just hatched, after eating most of its egg-shell as its first meal.

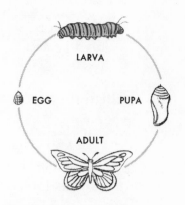

Hungry Orphans

Soon after laying her eggs, the mother butterfly or moth usually dies; often the father insect has died before. Then, with no parents to help them, the little orphan caterpillars have to make their way alone into the world.

The newly hatched caterpillar gives a final push. At last it is free. It has snipped a tiny lid out of its eggshell, and crawled out through the hole. Now it turns and makes its first meal of that same shell. Then it starts off on its strange little life.

Some people call caterpillars "worms."

What is a larva? Others call them "slugs," especially the slug cater-pillars which seem to glide along with no legs at all. The flat, thin types that tunnel through leaves are called leaf miners. A name that fits all caterpillars, however, is the term "larva." Cutworms, slug-caterpillars and leaf miners are all larvae. No matter how different they may appear, they all appear to have one purpose in life. They seem to want to eat as much as they possibly can.

A larva may eat almost without stopping from one sunrise to the next. Since it gets its air through the spiracles in its sides, it doesn't even need to stop to breathe. Resting right on the edge of a leaf, it stretches its head as far as it can reach. Then, clip, clip, clip go the little jaws like a pair of shears. It brings its head down towards its front legs, eating as it goes. Each time it cuts deeper into the leaf, eating everything but the large leaf-veins.

By the time a day has passed, it may **How much does a larva eat?** have eaten as much as its own body weight in food. If you weigh a hundred pounds, think of drinking twelve gallons of milk or eating seventy-five big loaves of bread every day!

All around the hungry little larva are hundreds of enemies. Birds and beetles search the leaves for insects. Lizards, bats, snakes, wasps and mice look for them. The larva, however, has only a few simple eyes down near the bottom of its helmet-shaped head. It cannot see all these enemies. Its stubby little antennae probably cannot detect them, either. How is it going to escape from all these dangers?

23

There are many ways in which nature has provided protection. Some of the larvae are colored the same as the plants on which they feed. Cabbage butterfly larvae are just as green as a cabbage leaf. Other caterpillars are colored like pieces of bark or twigs. Some measuring-worms look so much like twigs that they even have bumps resembling buds. When they are alarmed, they let go with their front legs and stick right out from the branch. There they stay motionless, like a little stub. Sometimes a bird will even try to alight on them.

How can a larva protect itself?

A few caterpillars are so bad-tasting that birds let them alone. The *milkweed* caterpillar, which will some day be a monarch butterfly, is one of them. Its bright colors of orange and black warn enemies to keep away (See illustration, page 16).

Other caterpillars are so fuzzy or hairy that they must taste like a mouthful of cotton. Fuzzy tent caterpillars are safe from most birds. So is the spiny larva of the mourning cloak butterfly. The cuckoo will eat them. It doesn't mind a mouthful of furry food.

A few larvae are really poisonous. The puss moth and saddleback caterpillars can cause a bad rash if you brush against their stinging hairs. Other caterpillars just act as if they were dangerous. When you touch a tomato hornworm, it flips back and forth as if to prick you with the spine at the end of its body. Actually, it is harmless. Probably it frightens many enemies this way.

One of the most interesting defenses is that of the tiger swallowtail larva. It has colored areas on its thorax which look like great, staring eyes. If this isn't frightening enough, it pokes two orange

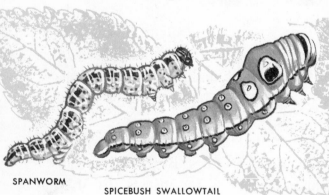

SPANWORM

SPICEBUSH SWALLOWTAIL

RED SPOTTED PURPLE

PUSS MOTH

fingerlike organs into the air from just behind its head. They have such an odd smell that an enemy really has to be hungry to eat it.

Mexican "jumping beans" are seeds with a little moth larva inside them. When the larva moves, the seed moves.

North America's largest caterpillar is the hickory horned devil. It is four inches long and covered with spines and spears. Although the spines are

Which are the largest and smallest larvae?

harmless, it looks so frightful that few enemies will touch it. It seems impossible that one day it will turn into the beautiful regal moth with its five-inch wingspan (See illustration, page 16).

Large as the horned devil is, however, it is small compared to some caterpillars of other continents. The larva of the Asian atlas moth is as big as a hot dog. The moth itself often has a wingspan of ten inches or more (See illustration, page 36).

Among the smallest caterpillars are the leaf miners. They are flat enough to tunnel through the leaf tissues. Their

Fuzzy Tent caterpillars are safe from most birds.

When in danger, the measuring worm imitates a twig.

The pattern of a leafminer's mine looks like a secret handwriting.

LEAFMINER CATERPILLAR

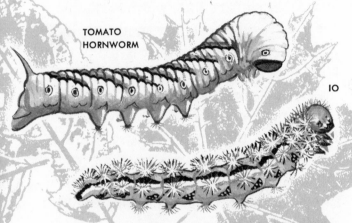

TOMATO HORNWORM

10

trails look like some strange kind of writing on the leaf. Once they were thought to be messages written by evil spirits. Some leaf-miner moths are so small that their outspread wings would not cover your little fingernail. Their little flat caterpillars are smaller than a pinhead.

What are case-bearers? There are little caterpillars called casebearers, which make a little case out of bits of leaf and other material. They carry this around with them wherever they go, like a snailshell. If

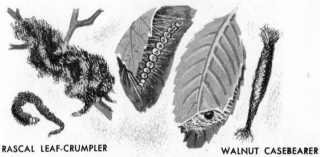

GRAPE LEAF FOLDER

RASCAL LEAF-CRUMPLER

WALNUT CASEBEARER

Coleophoridae (casebearers), with leaves and seeds.

it rains, they pull themselves inside their case as if it were a sleeping bag.

Some caterpillars cut circular pieces out of a large leaf. They live under this piece of leaf, which is like an umbrella. Still others roll a leaf around themselves for protection.

At left, a Golden-rod moth laying her eggs. At right, a cutaway of the gall, which is a swelling of the stem, showing the larva.

Gall caterpillars live inside the stems of plants. When the adult lays her eggs in the plant, the irritated tissue forms a growth around them, which we call a *gall*. The larva then lives inside this gall. Often these galls can be seen on the stems of dried weeds in the winter. If you cut them open you may still find the little insect larvae resting inside. Wasps, flies and other creatures also cause plants to make galls. Since the galls differ depending on the insect that caused them, you can tell the kind of larva inside by looking at the shape of the gall.

What causes plant galls?

Wherever most caterpillars go, they leave a silken trail. From a tiny opening in their lower lip comes a liquid, produced by a special gland, which hardens when it hits the air. It turns into a silk thread. Often, if a caterpillar falls, it is saved by the thread. The purpose of the gland and the thread is to provide the material used as protection when the caterpillar enters its next stage on the way of development into a butterfly or moth and for some other ways to protect the larva itself.

What is silk?

One of the most famous threads is that of the silkworm, the larva of an Asian moth. This caterpillar was first raised in Asia. Finally it was brought to Europe and America. The little worm eats mulberry leaves. Like all larvae, it splits its jacket several times until it is ready to become a pupa. Then it begins to spin.

How does the silkworm use its silk?

Its head goes back and forth, letting out more thread with each movement. It spins the thread around itself until it has made a whitish silk cocoon.

By carefully unwinding the silk, man can get a single strand, sometimes half a mile long. Then it is twisted with other strands into silk thread for cloth.

This wonderful material, mentioned several times in the Bible, has been known for more than 4000 years. Even with nylon and rayon taking the place of silk today, the shining cloth is still valuable. It takes almost 3000 silkworms to make a single pound of silk.

The tent caterpillar makes a nest of its silk. Dozens of these little campers stay in their tent-nest each night and then follow the silk trail out to the leaves in the day.

How else do larvae use their silk?

Birds sometimes take a piece of their nest to weave into their own nests.

Some caterpillars live underground in silk-lined tunnels. Underwater caterpillars sometimes make silk nets to hold a bubble of air. Like little skin-divers, they have their own air-tank with them.

The great scientist Jean Henri Fable discovered that some caterpillars are lost without their silk road. They cannot leave it any more than a train can leave its tracks. Once he made a number of processionary caterpillars march around in a circle. Each one followed the other for more than a week. They finally became so tired that they got "out of step" and were unable to keep up. Then they had to start out on uncertain journeys of their own.

Have you ever seen a flying caterpillar?

What is a flying caterpillar? Although they don't have wings, a few tiny caterpillars can sail through the air. Some let out a long silk thread until the wind catches it. Then they go floating away like a balloon. The gypsy moth larvae are so fuzzy that a puff of wind may carry them for thirty miles like a piece of thistledown. Scientists have found caterpillars high on snow-capped mountains. They had been carried there by the wind.

Most caterpillars have a tendency to crawl upwards, because the leaves they **Why do caterpillars crawl upward?** eat are usually on the ends of branches high in the tree. You can illustrate this

The fall Webworm and the Asian silkworm make silk suitable for thread; the silk of other larvae is less useful to us.

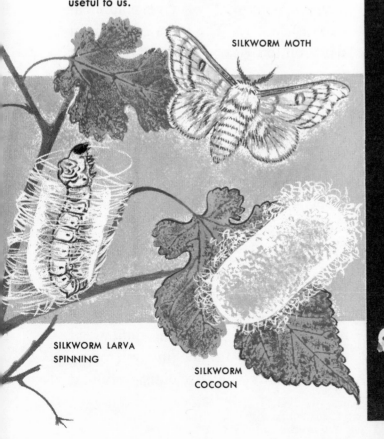

SILKWORM MOTH

SILKWORM LARVA SPINNING

SILKWORM COCOON

LARVA HANGING ON SILK THREAD

GOOSEBERRY SPANWORM

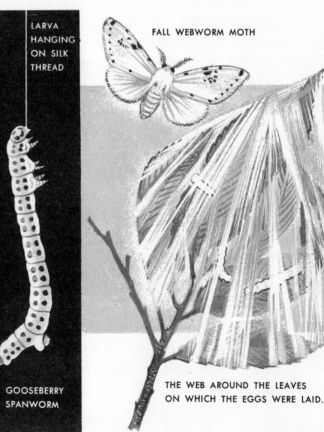

FALL WEBWORM MOTH

THE WEB AROUND THE LEAVES ON WHICH THE EGGS WERE LAID.

Above, a Tomato Hornworm caterpillar with parasitic wasp cocoons.
At right, an Ichneumon wasp laying
her eggs in the larvae of the Red
Humped appleworm.

tendency with a simple experiment. Let a caterpillar crawl up a stick you are holding. When it gets to the top, turn the stick upside-down so the caterpillar suddenly finds itself at the bottom. Away it will go, heading for the top again. When it has reached the top, turn it over once more. It starts right in to climb again.

How long will it continue to climb upwards? Probably as long as you feel like turning the stick. Scientists have tried it, and nearly always the scientist became tired before the caterpillar did.

When a number of caterpillars are eating at once, they can actually be heard. One of the most dreaded sounds on some farms is the steady crunching of thousands of army worms. They march across a hayfield or garden, eating almost every green thing in their path. Their busy jaws sound like a light breeze in the meadow.

**LARVA OF
CLOTHES
MOTH**

WAXMOTH

Not all caterpillars eat leaves. Perhaps

**What strange
things do
larvae eat?**

you have lost a good wool sweater because of wool caterpillars or clothes moths. Bee-keepers know that wax caterpillars can ruin a bee hive. The larva of the wanderer butterfly eats aphids or plant-lice.

Sometimes a caterpillar can be seen

**What insect
enemies do cater-
pillars have?**

with many little white objects on it. These are cocoons of tiny wasps. The wasp pokes her eggs into the caterpillar with her ovipositor. The little larvae hatch and eat the caterpillar's tissues. Then they make their cocoons on the outside of its skin. Flies, too, may attack caterpillars. These insect enemies are worth millions of dollars to the farmer in controlling harmful pests. Many scientists say that

**SILK TUNNEL OF
WAXMOTH LARVA**

they are even more effective than poisonous sprays or dusts. Since their work goes on unseen, however, we rarely notice them.

To care for caterpillars, you must keep them well supplied **How do you care for caterpillars?** with plenty of leaves. These may be placed with their stems in a jar of water. Be sure you have the same kind of leaves as those which the insects were eating when you caught them. Pack cotton or tissue paper so the caterpillars will not fall in the water.

As long as they have plenty to eat, the caterpillars will probably stay on the leaves. Sometimes it may be necessary to put a big piece of cheesecloth over them if they begin to wander. A large box with one side screened in may also be used. It is best to have a home for them before you start. Very few mothers like to chase caterpillars all over the house.

By the time a caterpillar is full grown, it has moulted, or changed its jacket, at least four times. Now it is ready to form a pupa. The days of crawling and eating are over.

The "Sleeping Puppet"

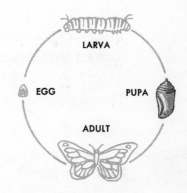

LARVA

EGG   PUPA

ADULT

There is a soft "plop, plop" in the forest. It sounds as if the trees were dripping after a rain. It is really the sound of larvae dropping to the ground. In other trees, larvae are lowering themselves slowly on their silken lifeline. Some larvae crawl down the stems of plants, or burrow into the ground.

They are no longer interested in food. The time has come for them to become a pupa. Some caterpillars may take days to find just the right spot. Other kinds merely settle down in the fork of a tree. Not all caterpillars enter the pupal

stage at the same time. New pupae develop every day, as new larvae become old enough.

Many moth caterpillars make a *cocoon*, **How does a moth make its cocoon?** while butterfly caterpillars make a similar structure, called a *chrysalis*. To build its cocoon, the caterpillar often starts by

29

making a soft, silken mattress. Standing on this, it weaves its head back and forth, around and around. With each movement, the strand of silk is pulled from the silk-gland on its lower lip. Gradually, the wall gets thicker. Finally the busy little spinner can hardly be seen inside its little room.

This is one way in which the cocoon is made. There are about as many other ways as there are moths. Many cocoons are beautifully formed, with ribs and cross-strands like fine lace. The *cecropia* moth caterpillar makes a cocoon of silk so tough that it is almost impossible to tear it. It may be larger than a hen's egg.

Other moth caterpillars roll themselves in a leaf. Bits of dirt, bark, and even the old larval skin may be woven into the cocoon. These materials help to hide and protect them. Once the caterpillar has become a pupa inside its cocoon, it is completely helpless.

The pupa of a butterfly is not covered

Why is a chrysalis called a golden pupa?

with silk. Usually it is very hard and shell-like. It may be shaped like a twig or piece of bark so that it is hard to see. The name chrysalis means golden. Often butterfly chrysalises are gold in color, or have gold beads and ornaments.

Just before its last moult, a change

How does a larva become a pupa?

comes over the caterpillar. It humps its back and pulls in its legs. If it becomes a chrysalis, it may hang down from a twig, holding on by hooks at the end of its body. If these lose their grip, it falls helplessly to the ground.

Finally the larval skin splits for the last time. Out pushes a strange new creature. Blind, with no legs for walking or wings for flying, it can move only by twisting its abdomen. It is a pupa at last, protected by the silken cocoon or the shell-like covering.

The name pupa means puppet in scientific language. If you look closely at a pupa, you will see that it looks like a little doll or puppet. It may be compared to a mummy, because the outlines of the new legs can be seen as if they were tightly wrapped in bandages, like a mummy. You can also see the wing pads, and the covers of the long mouth and antennae.

Now the pupa can do nothing but wait. It cannot take any food. It cannot drink. If even the smallest ant nibbles at it, it has no defense except its heavy coating. If dust gets into its spiracles, it may suffocate. It is as helpless as a person tied with rope from head to foot.

Some *sphinx* caterpillars burrow be-

Where can pupae be found?

neath the ground. There, the dark pupa, looking like a little jug with a handle, is hidden from sight. The puss moth pupa is covered over with the stinging hairs of the larva, so it is safe. Many pupae are tucked beneath bark, under stones, and under the edges of roofs. Some hang right out on a branch all winter, wrapped in an old leaf. They look so natural that nothing bothers them.

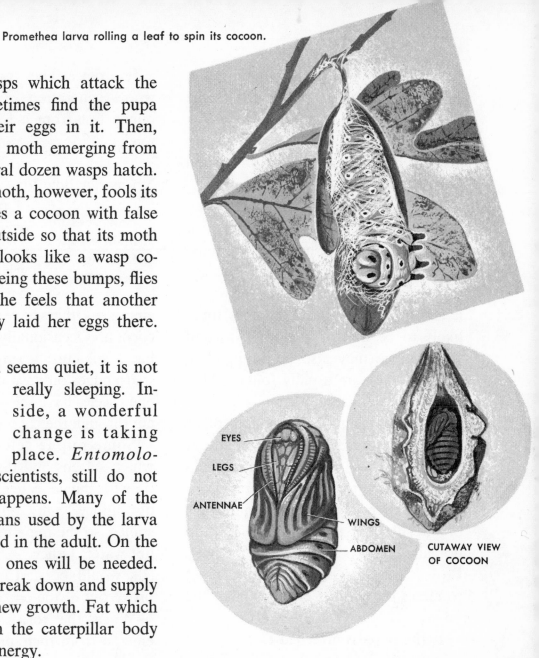

The little wasps which attack the caterpillars sometimes find the pupa also and lay their eggs in it. Then, instead of a new moth emerging from the cocoon, several dozen wasps hatch.

One African moth, however, fools its enemies. It makes a cocoon with false bumps on the outside so that its moth cocoon actually looks like a wasp cocoon. A wasp, seeing these bumps, flies away. Perhaps she feels that another wasp has already laid her eggs there.

Although a pupa seems quiet, it is not really sleeping. Inside, a wonderful change is taking place. *Entomologists,* or insect scientists, still do not know all that happens. Many of the muscles and organs used by the larva will not be needed in the adult. On the other hand, new ones will be needed. The old organs break down and supply their energy for new growth. Fat which was stored up in the caterpillar body is also used for energy.

What change takes place inside a pupa?

EYES

LEGS

ANTENNAE

WINGS

ABDOMEN

CUTAWAY VIEW OF COCOON

Some of the tissues, however, cannot be used at all. Yet if they stay in the body, they will be nothing but waste material. How does the pupa get rid of them?

The answer is found in tiny cells of the blood, called *phagocytes* (*FAG-o-sites*). These act like little scavengers. They eat up all unwanted material. Then they leave behind just what the insect needs.

The parasitic wasp egg has developed inside the pupa of a butterfly and now hatches.

If you find a pupa in the winter, it can

How can you keep a pupa? be preserved in the same way as the insect eggs. Be sure to make a note of where and when you found it.

Beetles and some other insects also form a pupa. You can tell the pupa of a moth or butterfly, however, by looking for the outline of the long, straight tube-mouth or proboscis. Of course if it is wrapped in silk, a pupa is quite likely to be that of a moth. Ant and wasp pupae may also be wrapped in silk, but they are usually found in the nests of these insects.

To keep a pupa for hatching, place it in a gallon jar with a wide mouth. A little paper towel in the bottom will help to hold moisture. Supply several drops of water every few days, allowing some of it to splash on the pupa. However, do not allow the bottom to get too wet. Provide a branch or stick for the insect to climb on when it emerges from the pupa.

PHOEBE FRITILLARY CHRYSALIS

If the pupa is attached to a support such as a twig, bring this in too. Then, when the moth emerges, it can crawl away and leave the pupal case behind. Otherwise, the case might stick to it when it moves around.

MONARCH CHRYSALIS

The process of change from pupa to

How long does an insect remain a pupa? adult may take months or even years. In a very dry year, some adults may not emerge at all, but wait for the following season. Others, such as the cabbage butterfly, may take only

a few days. They may go through a whole generation in a month. Many pupae last from a few days to a few weeks.

No matter how long it takes, the time

How does the moth escape from its cocoon? of pupation is finally over. Some cocoons have a little plug which the moth pushes out as it emerges. Others have a weak spot in the cocoon. Occasionally, the new insect has a silk-cutting ridge on its back or sharp edges on its wings. The pupae of one species have scissor-like jaws which cut through the cocoon.

Some pupae release a substance which softens and dissolves the silk in time for the delicate adult to leave without injury. Silkworms have this substance, so the pupa must be killed with hot water. Otherwise the fine strand of silk would be destroyed as the moth broke out of the cocoon.

When the tortoise-shell butterflies emerge from their pupae, they release a red substance. Sometimes many of them emerge at once. All these drops of reddish material look like a red rain dropping down from roofs and trees. Superstitious people used to call this a shower of blood. They often thought it meant the end of the world. Of course, it was really the beginning of a new life for the butterflies.

When finally the great day arrives, the industrious moth, which went into its closet in its work clothes, is ready to emerge and it will wear its best party dress.

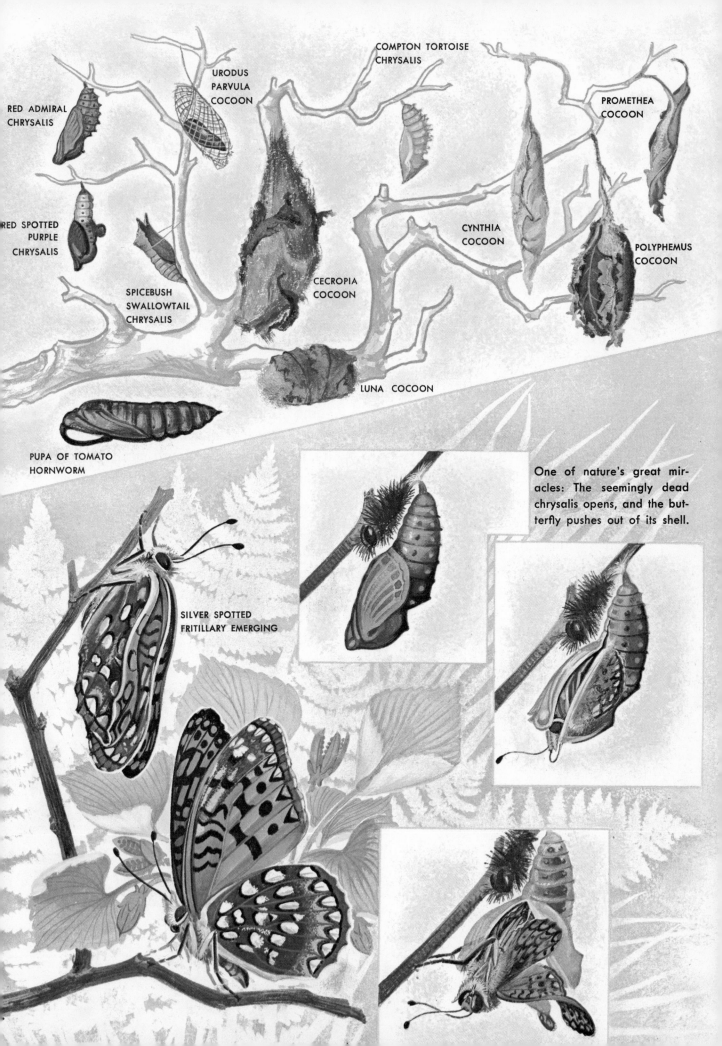

RED ADMIRAL
CHRYSALIS

URODUS
PARVULA
COCOON

COMPTON TORTOISE
CHRYSALIS

PROMETHEA
COCOON

RED SPOTTED
PURPLE
CHRYSALIS

CYNTHIA
COCOON

POLYPHEMUS
COCOON

SPICEBUSH
SWALLOWTAIL
CHRYSALIS

CECROPIA
COCOON

LUNA COCOON

PUPA OF TOMATO
HORNWORM

SILVER SPOTTED
FRITILLARY EMERGING

One of nature's great mir-
acles: The seemingly dead
chrysalis opens, and the butterfly pushes out of its shell.

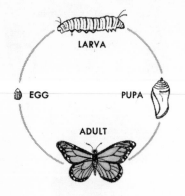

LARVA

EGG   PUPA

ADULT

"Flowers That Fly"

The chrysalis has been turning darker every day. When it was first formed, it was a pale green, with flecks of gold. Hanging partly by its tail and partly by a silken safety belt around its middle, it has remained quietly through the winter months. Now the spring sun shows the darkening of the yellow wings in their cases. The little pupa which seemed almost transparent at first, becomes brownish as the body colors darken.

Why does a chrysalis change color?

At last the hour is at hand. A split appears at the head end of the chrysalis. The body of the butterfly, wet and straining, forces it wider. It wriggles forward by twisting its abdomen.

How does the butterfly emerge from its chrysalis?

One by one the six legs pull out of their cases. The long proboscis, still uncoiled, begins to come free. The butterfly antennae with their little knobs draw away from their covering. The crumpled wings, wet and floppy, pull out of their pads.

As a green larva on a clover plant, its near-sighted eyes were almost useless. It could see little more than the difference between light and dark. If it had been starving, it couldn't have recognized a clover plant a few inches away. Now, however, it has great compound eyes. The little sulfur butterfly — for that is what it is — can see the world for the first time.

It sees the brightness of the May sunshine. It takes a first step with those brand-new legs. Then it carefully curls its new proboscis-mouth until it is a coiled tube. Its new antennae sample

the air. They tell it of a hundred fascinating new odors.

Slowly it fans those funny-looking wings up and down. Pumping air and a hardening substance into their veins, it gradually forces them into their new shape. With each slow fanning, the wings become larger and flatter.

Finally they spread out full-size toward the sun. They are no longer funny-looking, but a bright orange-yellow with a velvety black border. The body, clothed with yellow and black hairs, rests gracefully on the slender legs.

The sulfur butterfly doesn't glance at the empty chrysalis behind her. With a flip of her four wings she rises into the air. In a moment she seems to become a part of the golden sunshine. The little green caterpillar has turned into a butterfly.

The Indians once said that human beings were like caterpillars on earth. Often they buried their dead on platforms in the air in hope that their spirits could fly away as easily as the butterfly emerges from its pupa. The butterfly is sometimes used as a Christian symbol of resurrection, because it rises from a pupa that appears dead.

The little sulfur butterfly has close relatives over most of **Why do butterflies have "puddle parties"?** the world. The cabbage butterfly is one of the most familiar. It looks like a faded sulfur species. It often has "puddle parties" with

Puddle parties make sociable drinkers out of different butterflies.

35

many other kinds of butterflies. Dr. Alexander B. Klots, who has studied butterflies and moths as a life work, calls them "mud puddle clubs." They seem to be formed because the butterflies like the moisture at the edge of a rain puddle, and gather there to drink.

The period after a shower is one of the best times to see butterflies and moths. Not only do they come out of hiding, but many pupae will open up in damp weather.

Pupae open at all hours of the day and nearly all days of the year, except in northern regions, where they open only during the short summer. Many species have two or three generations each year. The larva of the early spring mourning cloak may feed on new forest leaves. By midsummer, they have grown to adults. Their larvae, in turn, will be seen by fall.

Often we think of moths and but-

terflies just as insects with wonderful colors. However, they also have unusual habits like the larvae. For instance, there are butterflies that "hitch" rides. There are moths that can fly backwards. There are moths that have no wings. And who ever heard of a butterfly fight? Yet some butterflies chase each other. They will even chase birds and human beings, although they could not possibly harm them.

Primitive people sometimes call butterflies and moths the *flowers that fly*. They have as many colors as the thousands of jungle blooms. There are red butterflies and moths, blue ones, pink ones, white ones. There are brown ones, rainbow ones, and even black ones. Some have spots on the wings like great staring eyes. Others have tails on the wings that may be ten inches long.

Why do male butterflies wear perfume?

Some moths and butterflies even have flower-like scents. The males of a number of species have little perfume-scales on their wings or legs. These serve to attract the females. As they wave their wings, the perfume is spread on the breeze.

The natives of some Pacific islands wear living butterflies carefully tied in their hair. The waving wings of the insect must make a startling sight. Even more startling, however, must be a butterfly kite.

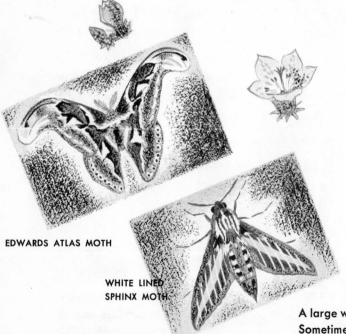

EDWARDS ATLAS MOTH

WHITE LINED SPHINX MOTH

A large wing span does not always guarantee speed. Sometimes the smaller "brothers" are faster flyers.

BIRDWING BUTTERFLY

CECROPIA MOTH

HUMMINGBIRD MOTH

One of the few insects that can fly backwards.

A Pacific Island native with a live butterfly in her hair.

To make a butterfly kite, natives of the East Indies use bird-wing butterflies, which often have a wingspan of nearly ten inches. The

What is a butterfly kite?

butterflies are tied to a string. Then children walk along with the butterflies sailing around above them like a kite in the wind.

The hummingbird sphinx flies to a flower. Hovering in the air on its rapidly-beating wings,

What moth can fly backwards?

it uncoils its long proboscis to reach the nectar. Then it backs away and goes to another flower. It is one of the few insects that can fly backwards.

Although the bird-wings can fly well, huge moths and butterflies are not always the best fliers. The twelve-inch Edwards

How fast do moths and butterflies fly?

atlas moth of the Himalayas is one of the largest moths known, but it is slower than a four-inch hawk moth. Some kinds of hawk moths have wingbeats so fast that they are just a blur.

Some hawk moths can fly thirty miles per hour. This is faster than many birds. Most moths and butterflies are much slower. They usually can fly about as fast as a person can run. Often, if they are being chased, they will turn and let the wind carry them away. In this way they can swiftly escape their enemies.

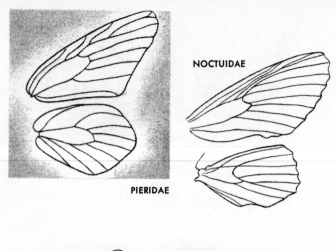

NOCTUIDAE

PIERIDAE

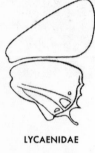

LYCAENIDAE

SPHINGIDAE

AEGERIIDAE

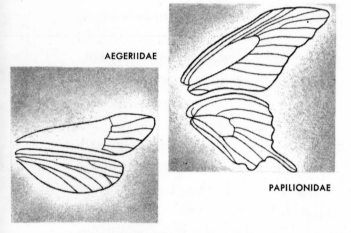

PAPILIONIDAE

The veins in the wings of butterflies and moths indicate the families to which the insects belong.

Why do wings have veins in them?
At first glance the wing veins seem to be scattered over the wing. However, they are really arranged in a regular order, giving the wing much support. Although called veins, they do not just carry blood, like our veins. They are stiff hollow rods, each of which has a scientific name. Entomologists can tell the family of a moth or butterfly by carefully looking at the veins. There are several dozen families, each with different wing veins.

What do the adults eat?
The larvae eat green leaves, but most butterfly and moth adults feed only on liquids. Although we usually see them on flowers gathering nectar, they also visit moist ground and even garbage heaps. A very few have chewing jaws and feed on pollen.

The coiled proboscis lets a moth or butterfly sip nectar from the deepest flowers. One scientist found a jungle flower ten inches deep. He was convinced that there must be a moth which could feed from such a flower, although none was known. Sure enough, one was found some time later. It was a giant hawk moth with a proboscis ten inches long — twice the length of its body.

How long do they live?
Some moths, like the cecropia, eat nothing at all. They live on food stored in their bodies as a larva. Such moths live only for a few days. Most summer moths and butterflies live about a month as adults.

If these insects had no means of protection as they flew through the air, they would soon be killed. How do such brightly-colored insects manage to survive? There are as many ways as there are insects, for each species has its own special method.

The little skippers get their name from

What colors can they see?

their quick, dancing flight. Skippers and other butterflies have been known to fly to the colored shoulder patches of soldiers at attention. Perhaps these bright colors seemed like flowers to them. They were most likely attracted by yellow, blue or green; most butterflies are not affected by red.

Although moths hide from the very

Do moths really fly toward lights?

bright sunlight, they are attracted to open flames or a hot electric light. (Even a bright electric light is dimmer than the sun.) Many moths, not realizing the danger from the very hot light, will flutter around it until they are burned to death. The muscles of a moth are influenced by light. The side toward the light is weakened, and tends to involuntarily turn toward the light.

There are no muscles in the wing of any

How many muscles do insects have?

insect. They are found inside the thorax. The end of the wing projects into the thorax, and the strong muscles work it up and down,

CLOUDY WING SKIPPER

SILVER SPOTTED SKIPPER

something like the oar of a boat. Scientists have found 4,000 muscles in the bodies of some insects. There are only about 500 muscles in our own bodies.

Some butterflies survive because of their

How do moths and butterflies protect themselves?

bad taste. One of these is the monarch butterfly. By advertising its taste with bold orange and black colors, it tells enemies to leave it alone. After they have tried one or two monarch butterflies, they pay no more attention to them.

Without the Yucca moth laying her eggs in the base of the yucca flower, no yucca plants would be pollinated. Without the yucca plant providing food for the yucca moth larvae, no yucca moths could develop. This is a case of mutual dependence.

Yucca seed with larva inside. Indentation shows spot where the larva is feeding.

The Viceroy (right) looks like the Monarch (left).

YELLOW BANDED UNDERWING RESEMBLING BARK

HORNET MOTH

The underside of the Dead Leaf butterfly is difficult to distinguish from a dead leaf.

The little viceroy butterfly is orange and black too. Even though it is not bad-tasting, it looks so much like the monarch that birds take no chances. They let it alone, too. By this process, called mimicry, many harmless butterflies look like other species that have disgusting tastes and odors.

What is mimicry?

Butterflies and moths often look like other objects around them. The dead-leaf butterfly has veins and brown color like an old leaf. It even has a point like a leaf stem.

How do insects use camouflage?

Its enemies may look right at it without seeing it. Other moths and butterflies are colored like bark, flowers, or grass. When they are resting on such places, they are hard to find. The coloration which hides the insect is called camouflage.

On some moths the hind wings are quite different in color from the front pair. These are called *underwing* moths. As they fly, the bright hind pair makes them easily seen. When they light on a tree or stone and fold their wings, only the gray upper pair is visible. The bright hind wings are hidden, and the insects seem to disappear.

The Cloudless Sulphur looks very much like the yellow flowers on which it feeds.

Resting by day, the Clouded Locust hides its bright-colored underwings under its upper wings, which resemble the bark of locust trees.

The courtship dance of the butterflies (Buckeyes in our picture) is a familiar sight in the warm months.

Other bright colors confuse enemies. There are so many patches and spots on some species that it is hard to believe they are just one insect. Their bright spots look like patches of light. When they rest on a shady leaf they seem to be only a little spot of sunlight.

The mourning cloak butterfly has brownish-blue wings with light borders. They are dull on the underside. When it suddenly alights and folds them above its back, one can hardly discover where it is resting. Other butterflies play possum. They fall to the ground with folded wings and then lie among the leaves as if dead until danger has passed. They are so good at fooling their enemies with this game that they can even be picked up and carried away without moving themselves.

Why do some moths and butterflies have strange shapes?

Butterflies and moths may have confusing shapes. They may be shaped like broken pieces of leaves with scalloped edges and even make-believe worm holes. Wasp moths are colored and shaped like a stinging wasp. Rolled-wing moths curl their wings around themselves so they look like a dead twig.

41

Butterflies and moths sometimes chase each other around in a courtship dance. A few make buzzing or crackling sounds as they fly. Sometimes a male will fight with another male, although it is hard to see how they could hurt each other. A male may chase a piece of paper blowing along the ground, mistaking it for a competitor. It may also chase birds, dogs or even people.

What is a butterfly dance?

After the flying flowers have mated, the female is ready to lay her eggs. Sometimes she lays them at once, in a single mass. Other times she waits for days. If she belongs to a species that remains dormant through the winter, she will not lay them until the following spring.

At last the job of the adults is done. They have left their eggs behind. Soon their lifeless bodies drop to the ground. The other adults which will wait until spring to lay their eggs prepare to find a place to rest. So do many larvae and pupae.

Winter vacation is about to begin.

Winter Vacation

All during the late summer the monarch butterfly has circled lazily above the fields. Its warning orange and black coloring has shielded it from the birds. It seems to have little to do but visit the flowers. Really, however, it is getting ready to begin an amazing journey.

One day it lifts itself on the breeze. Instead of circling lazily, it picks out a definite direction. Now its wings beat with a new purpose.

It heads toward the south. Almost as if it knew the summer would soon end, it starts for a warmer country. Mile after mile it goes. It passes over farmers in the hayfields. It flies over cities and towns. Birds fly close and look it over. They decide not to disturb it.

At night, the butterfly comes to rest on a branch. Sometimes it is joined by thousands of other monarchs. They give an entire tree a strange new crop of orange "leaves."

The next day it is off again. With no road maps or guides of any kind to be seen, it keeps on its way. If it comes to a lake, or even a bay of the ocean, it fearlessly starts out across it.

Sometimes it goes a hundred miles in a day. Sometimes winds and rain hold it back. It keeps on, however, until it reaches the southland. This may be Florida, California or even Mexico.

How far does the monarch butterfly go in winter?

It stays there most of the winter. Then it starts north again. Scientists used to think it made the same trip back again. Now they think it often goes only part way. Finally it stops and lays its eggs on a milkweed. The new caterpillars hatch out. In a few weeks they are adults, and continue the journey north. It is almost as if the butterfly generations were running a great relay race, with each one starting out where the last one stopped.

The monarch migration is one of the best known insect voyages. Sometimes hundreds of them will go past a certain spot in a day.

Where is "butterfly park"?

At Pacific Grove, California, as many as two-million sometimes rest in the trees. A special butterfly park has been set aside for them.

This is one of the few places where butterflies are protected. In South America, Brazil found it necessary to protect its big blue morpho butterflies. So many collectors wanted them that the government had to pass a law to save them.

Other butterflies migrate as well. The little sulfur butterfly may travel a few miles. Even the mourning cloak sometimes takes a winter vacation south of its summer home. Some butterflies just go to a sheltered valley for the winter.

Butterflies can travel as far as two hundred miles out to sea. If a ship passes below, they may alight on its deck. Sometimes they remain there for

How far can moths and butterflies travel?

the rest of the voyage. Such little hitchhikers spread a species of butterfly or moth to far-away countries. Monarch butterflies getting aboard a ship at California may get off at Hawaii or Japan. Such pests as the Oriental fruit moth and the European corn borer come to America in this way.

People sometimes try to tell what kind of a winter it will be by looking at the creatures around

Can animals predict weather?

them. Such creatures are sometimes called weather prophets. Hunters say that if a squirrel's tail is very bushy it will be a cold winter. Farmers say that the thicker a cow's coat the harder the winter will be. Even the hair on cater-

SOUTH AMERICAN MORPHO
NOW PROTECTED BY LAW

MIGRATING MONARCH BUTTERFLIES

pillars is supposed to tell something about the weather.

Look carefully in the fall at the woolly bear caterpillar. Its fuzzy body is brown in the middle and black at both ends. Some people say that a wide center band means a winter with little snow. The caterpillar, of course, cannot really predict the weather. But every year, people have fun guessing. (See illustration, page 16.)

In spite of what its coat is supposed to say about the weather, the woolly bear caterpillar just hides beneath a pile of dead leaves. There it remains until spring. With the arrival of spring it turns into a yellow-gray Isabella moth.

Why do insects sleep in winter?

Often people feel sorry for moths, butterflies and other insects which must stay out in the cold. Whether they are eggs, larvae, pupae or adults they have to stop all activity. However, even if they tried to keep going all winter, they could never do it. They would have no way to keep their bodies warm, for they are cold-blooded. There would be no leaves to eat, no flowers to visit. So do not feel sorry for a red admiral or painted lady butterfly hiding under a frosty ledge. Perhaps they are more comfortable in the homes they have made than you are as you stand in the snow and look at them.

Even in the tropics where there is no winter, many insects rest for days or weeks in the dry season. Winter is a period of rest, but one day it will be over. Then the moths, butterflies and their young will begin to stir. It will be time for the great awakening once again, in every climate.

SPECIMEN ENVELOPE
FROM FOLDED SHEET

Butterflies in a Box

Now that you have learned something about moths and butterflies, you may wish to make your own insect collection. Butterflies and moths make interesting wall decorations, and thousands of people make collecting them their lifetime hobby.

Where can you get collecting equipment?

There are many places where you can obtain collecting equipment. Most colleges and high schools can give you their addresses. There are even places where you can buy or trade specimens.

Some kinds of rare tropical moths and butterflies sell for as much as one hundred dollars each.

You don't need any money to get started in collecting, however. You don't even need to find a place that sells specimens. If you live in the country, moths and butterflies are all around you. Even in the city, they can be found in parks. They often fly around street lights at night.

One of the first things you need for collecting is a net. You

How can you make your own equipment?

can make this yourself with about five feet of heavy wire. Bend it into a circle, leaving two ends sticking out about eight-inches long.

Wire the two ends to a light, strong stick about three-feet long. If bamboo is available, the loop-ends can be stuck into its hollow center.

Sew a double layer of cheesecloth or diaper cloth into the shape of a bag about twenty-four inches deep on the loop. Then your net is ready to use.

A killing bottle is the next item. A wad of cotton can be soaked in carbon tetrachloride and dropped into an airtight glass bottle. Place a false bottom of cardboard over the cotton so the insects do not touch the moisture, as it will discolor them. Be sure the bottle is big enough for large-winged specimens.

After two or three minutes in the bottle the insects can be removed. If you cannot mount them right away, put

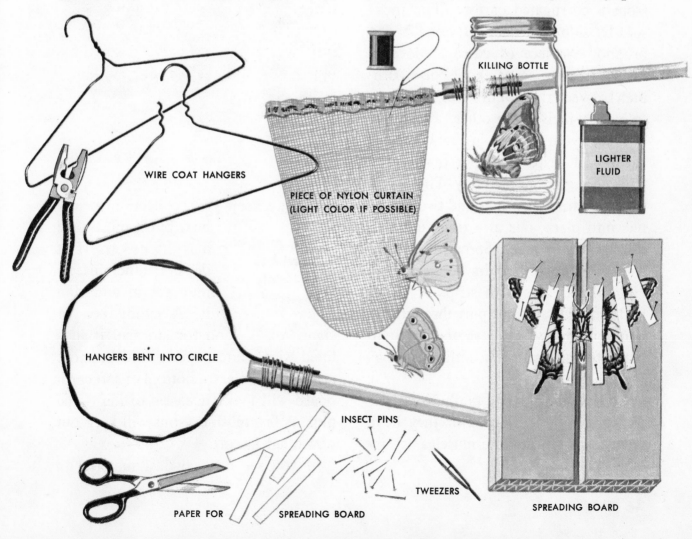

WIRE COAT HANGERS

PIECE OF NYLON CURTAIN (LIGHT COLOR IF POSSIBLE)

KILLING BOTTLE

LIGHTER FLUID

HANGERS BENT INTO CIRCLE

INSECT PINS

TWEEZERS

PAPER FOR SPREADING BOARD

SPREADING BOARD

them in little envelopes or folded pieces of paper. This will prevent their scales from rubbing off.

You will need pins to mount your specimens. Common pins will do, but perhaps a high school biology teacher can help you get some insect pins. They are thinner and longer. No. 1 and No. 2 pins are good for most insects. Place a pin straight down through the thorax of your butterfly. Push it until the insect is about three-quarters of the way up toward the pinhead.

How should insects be mounted?

To spread the wings, you will need a spreading board. Cut two strips about ten inches long and five inches wide from a corrugated carton. Glue these side by side to a flat soft wood board or another piece of corrugated cardboard. Leave a space about one-eighth-inch between them at one end, widening to half-an-inch at the other.

Place your insect in between the cardboard strips at a spot that is just wide enough to fit the body. Then carefully pull the four wings and two antennae into place, one at a time, until all are flat and straight. Spread the wings well so that both pairs can be seen. Hold them there with strips of paper and pins. Do not put pins through the wings themselves. Leave the moth in place for several days until the wings are firmly set.

Some butterflies and moths are easier to work with the day after they have been caught. Then the muscles are relaxed.

If a specimen has become "set" in the wrong position, it can be relaxed by placing it in a jar with moist cotton for a day. Put some moth crystals in with the cotton or mold can quickly form. You can also place your specimen in a sieve over hot water for a few minutes. Be careful not to damage the insect.

Be sure you put a little tag of paper on the pin, telling where and when you caught the insect. This is the mark of a good collector. Also put your name on the tag. A separate tag can be used for the name of the butterfly when you have identified it.

Life history set of Buck moth.

You may keep your collection in any box, but it must have a tight cover. If it doesn't, other insects may get in and ruin it. A candy box or cigar box is good for storage. If it is lined with white paper it will be more attractive. An extra bottom of soft cardboard will make it easier to insert the pins. A few moth crystals will keep out unwanted insects.

Why must an insect box be tightly covered?

If you see fine sawdust material in

your collection, put in more moth crystals at once. The sawdust probably indicates that carpet beetles are attacking your specimens. These are tiny black or brownish beetles. They can destroy a valuable collection in a few days.

You can make display mounts from your specimens. Supply houses sell Riker mounts, which are flat black boxes with glass tops. The box is filled with cotton on which you can place the

Life history set of Cabbage butterfly.

specimen so that it is clearly visible. Then the glass cover is put in place.

You can make your own mounts from

How can you make a display case?

a box, cotton, and glass. Seal the glass and box tightly with tape so that no insects can enter the box. Paint the box black, and glue a picture hook to its back. Then it can be hung on the wall.

The colors of moths and some butterflies will fade if exposed to light. Some, however, such as the blues, are caused by the way the light strikes the lines on the scales. These can be left in bright sunlight for years without fading. How-

ever, it is best to keep your collection covered when not in use, and your collection always appears fresh.

A popular collection is a "life history

How can you make a life history set?

set". This consists of all four stages of a moth or butterfly. Pin the eggs, pupa and adult to the bottom of a small box. The larva can be put in a small vial in rubbing alcohol solution. This will take the color out of the larva, but they seem to lose their colors after they have died, no matter what method is used. If possible, also include a piece of the plant on which the caterpillar feeds.

Butterfly collecting is a wonderful hobby. There is always a chance that you will find a specimen that is new. Many scientists feel that for every one that is now known there are five butterflies and moths still to be discovered. Even a beginner may someday have the thrill of finding a new species. This is one reason it is important to keep "where and when" labels on your specimens.

Collectors often spread a sheet out at

How can specimens be attracted?

night and shine a light on it. This makes a large bright area that attracts the moths. Sometimes a flashlight will "shine" the eyes of moths in the dark. They will reflect the light like the eyes of a dog or cat.

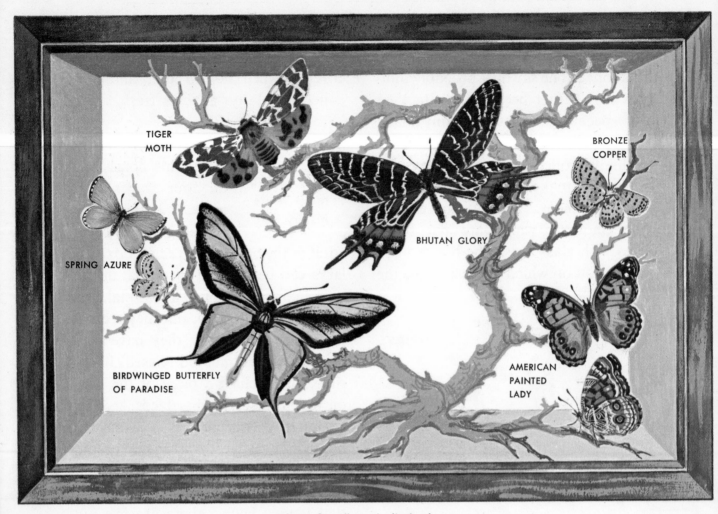

TIGER MOTH

BRONZE COPPER

SPRING AZURE

BHUTAN GLORY

BIRDWINGED BUTTERFLY OF PARADISE

AMERICAN PAINTED LADY

A butterfly collector's display box.

Butterflies will come to a dish of sweetened water or a bouquet of flowers on a window sill. Moths will come to the same window at night, especially if a light is burning.

One collector used to get moths from a window a few inches off the ground. Each night he would turn the light on at a certain time. Then he would collect insects for about an hour. One night he discovered that he had an unusual visitor. A frog, happening to come along at the right time, was feeding on the insects as they dropped from the window. Soon it learned to come every night. The collector had to be quicker than the frog in order to get the specimens he wanted.

In the jungle, some moths and butterflies stay high in the trees. Collectors have to shoot them down with guns using dust shot.

Watching, collecting, studying and reading about moths and butterflies is lots of fun. With 9,000 moths and butterflies known in America today, you will never run out of new insects and new stories to tell.